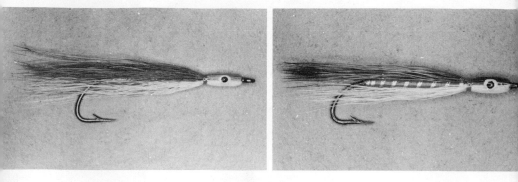

photographs by Matthew Vinciguerra

TYING AND FISHING THE
THUNDER CREEK
SERIES

KEITH
FULSHER

FRESHET
PRESS INC.
ROCKVILLE CENTER, NEW YORK

Brief quotations from this book may be used in critical reviews written for inclusion in a newspaper or magazine. For any other reproduction of any part of this book, however, written permission must be obtained from the publisher.

ISBN 0-88395-018-9

Library of Congress Card Number: 72-92787

Manufactured in the United States of America

Designed by Joan Stoliar

This book is dedicated to all the fly fishermen I have fished with over the years, but especially to Louie Hitzke and Ward Fulsher, who introduced me to Thunder Creek; to Pete Ceasrine, my constant fishing companion, and to Bob Sigsby; to Charlie Krom, the greatest fly tier I know, who is always generous with his creations and always easy to talk into a fishing trip; to Roger Menard, that fine fly-tier and recluse of the Catskills, who has shown me his secret fishing spots; to Al Zatorski, with whom I tied my first trout fly; to my son, Keith, Jr., who catches trout in the places where I tell him not to cast; to Frank Bondatti, my salmon-fishing partner and chef without equal, who always has a new and novel way to land a salmon; and to Mattie Vinciguerra, who deserves a special word of gratitude, not only for his companionship astream but also for the perfection he insisted upon in doing the photography for this book.

Contents

1 The Evolution of Flies That Imitate Baitfish 13

2 Developing and Testing a New Theory 19

3 How to Tie the Thunder Creek Series 27

4 The Thunder Creek Patterns and Their Living Counterparts 40

5 Reasons for Using Baitfish Imitations and Some Tackle Notes 77

6 Fly Selection and Fishing Techniques 87

7 Salt-Water Thoughts 93

8 Assuring the Future of Your Sport 97

introduction

The value of baitfish as a food source for game fish cannot be overemphasized, since baitfish, in their various species, represent the single most important item of food for the larger predators. Because of this fact, the baitfish imitation can be one of the most effective of the fly fisherman's lures, yet these long flies have never received anything like the attention that has been lavished on dry flies, wet flies, and nymphs. The colors, forms, and proportions of insect-imitation flies have been endlessly refined, but the baitfish-imitation fly-rod lures—streamers and bucktails—have remained basically unchanged over the years.

Game fish are known to often be selective in their dining habits when it comes to baitfish, though perhaps not as much so as they are with the various insects and stages of insect life. Nevertheless, they often do prefer one species of baitfish to another, and the serious fly fisher should take this selectivity into consideration. The purpose of this book is to show, through the development of my own Thunder Creek series of lures, that improvements in the design of baitfish imitations is possible and that there are good reasons for making these improvements along exact-imitation lines. I have concentrated mainly on fresh-water fly fishing, although in Chapter 7 I have touched on the adaptation of the Thunder Creek series to salt-water fly fishing.

A work of this nature reflects a personal view, of course, coming as it must from one's own associations and experiences, and certainly I don't offer my ideas as authoritative. The reader must decide for himself whether the thoughts advanced herein are sound enough to warrant his tying the patterns and trying them out. I'm fairly sure, though, that anglers who give them a trial will be pleased with the results.

1
The Evolution of Flies That Imitate Baitfish

A discussion of the different types of artificial lures used in fishing with a fly rod can very easily lead to the question of why bucktails and streamers, which are primarily baitfish imitations, are called *flies*. The obvious answer would seem to be that, inasmuch as baitfish imitations made of hair or feathers were developed long after artificial insects and the fly rod itself came into common use, it was natural enough for fishermen to refer casually to fly-rod baitfish imitations as flies, since they were tied and fished in much the same way as insect imitations. Do you agree? I'm not wholly convinced. There's no question in my mind that fly rods were developed to fish with insects, either natural or artificial, and that the later adaptation of baitfish imitations to the fly rod was the reason that these imitations came to be called flies. But it is my firm conviction that the first lures ever made of hair or feathers were fashioned in a simple

13

elongated shape that resembled a baitfish. Such lures, designed solely for the purpose of getting food, surely predated the fly rod and the artificial insect. The creation of artificial insects was a much later development, and although both types of lures were made in nearly the same way, it was with the artificial insect that the true sporting aspect of fishing arose. Sometime after the sporting concept took hold, imitations of baitfish, somewhat modified from their original form, were incorporated into the fly fisherman's list of "flies."

A significant case in point is the development of the bucktail called the Alaska Mary Ann, and although its origin is relatively recent, it evolved along the lines just mentioned. The earliest version of the lure was developed by Alaskan Eskimos. This consisted of an elongated body carved from bone with a few polar-bear hairs bound to the top to provide action and a crudely made copper hook anchored to the tail end of the body. This lure was obviously designed to look and act like a small fish. Frank Dufresne converted this lure into a regular fly-rod bucktail, replacing the bone body with ivory silk but retaining the polar-bear hair and maintaining the original color scheme. Today the Alaska Mary Ann is a very popular and successful fly.

Much of what has been written about artificial flies is concerned only with insect imitations. Nothing has been found in early fishing literature that would shed light on the origin of fly-rod baitfish imitations, so one theory is as good as the next. Maybe the art of simulating baitfish was thought to be too obvious to dwell upon when compared with the challenges offered in duplicating delicate insects. We know from *The Treatise of Fishing with an Angle* that insect imitations were well established in the fifteenth century. We also know from a fragment by the Roman writer Aelian that an insect imitation existed as early as the second century A.D., so the beginnings of fly-tying go back a long, long way. If my supposition that a form of streamer or bucktail predates the earliest insect imitations is correct, then the first efforts at primitive fly-tying date from far back in antiquity.

Many primitive societies must have developed lures similar to the one used by the Kobuk Eskimos that was the original for the Alaska Mary Ann. They had feathers and animal hair available to them as well as materials to make short, crude lines and hooks, and they were very adept at using these things. The implementation was easy—a short hair or fiber line was attached to a crude hook to which was bound a few animal hairs or feathers. However, the long flies also evolved in a much more recent and possibly even more important way. I'm referring to their evolution as fly-rod lures along with and as a result of the development of insect imitations. As fly-tiers became more proficient in their art, they expanded the scope of their imitations by attempting to copy a greater and greater variety of insects. Some of these insects, most notably stone flies and caddis flies, have long wings that extend back parallel to the body, and when fly-tiers made copies of these flies they produced an artificial that looked and acted more like a baitfish in the water than an insect. Even some of the standard wet-fly patterns have this effect when tied with exceptionally long hackles and wings. These flies were successful, and the idea caught on. Eventually, long-

15

winged flies were recognized as serving as baitfish imitations and were deliberately tied as such.

Since the late 1800s, fly-rod baitfish imitations in the form of bucktails and streamer flies have steadily increased in popularity. Maine guides and fishermen found the long flies to be much more productive in the cold lakes of Maine than all other fly-rod lures put together, and with good reason. Studies made over the years of the stomach contents of trout and landlocked salmon taken from Maine lakes indicate that about seventy-five per cent of the food these fish eat consists of small fish. Similar analyses in other lakes and reservoirs where trout and salmon abound would surely turn up similar results. These fish become primarily meat eaters once they reach the length of twelve inches.

Many of the Maine bucktail and streamer patterns, especially the earlier ones, are very long and run to bright colors. They are often tied on 8X-long hooks or on the longer tandem rigs that really stretch them out. These brilliant attractor patterns no doubt followed to some degree the very colorful wet-fly patterns that had been so successful with brook trout. Certainly they were not too representative of the coloring found in actual baitfish. Later, patterns were toned down and were dressed in the softer shades of real baitfish. This resulted in a variety of smelt patterns dressed in various shades of blue, green, and gray with a touch of other colors added. These flies worked very well, and some became famous. All reinforced the exact-imitation theory.

The success of bucktails and streamers in Maine led to their increased popularity all across the country, and today you can find these long flies in almost any fly fisherman's vest. Even some fishermen who don't use them enjoy making them because of their attractiveness, and you often see bucktails and streamers displayed on a sportsman's hat or fishing vest. I wouldn't be a bit surprised if even the dry-fly purists occasionally work one through a favorite pool when fish are sluggish and holding deep. Be that as it may, more and more fly-tiers are developing exact baitfish imitations, and some of the results have been impressive. It's not unusual for a new bucktail or streamer to run up enviable records and develop into a great pattern of world-wide use. Such a fly can be used successfully under a greater variety of conditions than any other type.

In recent years Lew Oatman made some great strides toward developing flies to imitate specific species of baitfish. Lew was a professional who specialized in feather-wing streamer patterns, and every one of his creations was a work of art. He was a leader in reducing the size of streamers and using sparse dressings with short wings. Because of these modifications, his streamers are particularly successful in small and heavily fished streams. He also set the pace by toning down the colors in his work to imitate the natural shadings of small shiners and darters. His flies were remarkably effective and were quickly accepted by the fishing public. The exceptional progress Lew was making in the field of baitfish imitation was cut short by his untimely death, but the dozen and a half patterns that he developed will long remain favorites of fishermen who prefer close copies of natural baitfish.

I strongly believe in the exact-imitation theory and feel that to look more natural a baitfish imitation must have good color simulation and all of the dominant physical characteristics of the fish being copied. It must also have a lifelike action in the water. Baitfish imitations are fished beneath the surface, where the fish have an opportunity to look them over carefully, so these things become even more important than they are in the case of the dry fly.

We are living in a time of great fishing pressure and diminishing fishing places. Refinement of fly-fishing tackle and the flies themselves must continually be made to keep pace with the increasing demands on our sport fish. These fish, many of which are caught and released a number of times during their lives, owing to the generosity of a new breed of fly fishermen, are developing a greater awareness and are very difficult to catch on unnatural-looking flies of any type, even though these same patterns may have a history of producing well. These conditions create a strong case for exact imitation, and it is with baitfish imitations that the greatest improvements of this sort can be made.

2
Developing and Testing a New Theory

Most fly fishermen have had the experience of standing in a quiet pool on a favorite stream when suddenly a good-sized trout goes on a feeding spree. He doesn't rise delicately to floating insects and usually he won't look at a wet fly or nymph. His interest is meat in the form of smaller fish. He will race from one end of the pool to the other, almost charging out on the bank, and will sometimes flash in the water right beside your boots as he catches and engulfs a hapless minnow. He will carry on his erratic action for a few minutes, then all will become quiet and it will seem as if there isn't a fish in the pool. If it's a small pool, the wildly feeding trout may well have chased the others out or at least driven them into hiding places, so that fishing will be slow for a good long time. Several times when this happened to me I unsuccessfully tried every fly in my fly box that was meant to imitate a minnow. These failures set me to thinking about the design and tying methods of the conventional bucktails and streamers that I was using.

If a reasonably exact imitation of a baitfish was desired, several obvious changes in design seemed necessary. Most important, a more natural-looking head was called for. A minnow's head usually represents about one fifth of its entire length, give or take a bit. The eyes are of generous size and are located in about the center of the head. On many species, though, they are positioned slightly above and forward of center. These facts are not taken into consideration in the tying of most conventional patterns. The usual bucktails and streamers are made with small heads that are only slightly built up with tying thread, and the eyes are either missing entirely or misrepresented by jungle-cock feathers, which do not fall in the proper place to represent eyes. Some patterns call for small lacquer eyes to be painted on the tying thread after the head wrappings are complete, and although this is a reasonable idea, such eyes look unnaturally squeezed in because the head is much too small.

The back and belly colors of a live minnow usually carry smoothly from nose to tail with only slight shading variations along the minnow's length, regardless of what kind of markings the fish carries on its sides. Most artificials break off the color scheme sharply where the head is formed with tying thread. Sometimes colored lacquers are used to shade the thread wrappings of the head, but this does not entirely solve the problem.

Another thing to consider in attempting to produce a fairly exact copy of a baitfish had to do with the dimensions of the real thing. The dimensions of the natural are extremely difficult to produce using conventional tying methods and the basic hairs and feathers normally associated with fly-tying. This is especially true when elongated hackle wings are used. Length and height present no problem, of course, but width, which is necessary to give an impression of the oval body of the natural, is much harder to fabricate. The tapered bodies of conventionally tied bucktails and streamers can be made to approximate the desired shape, but when these flies are fished slowly, especially when they are sinking or being gradually moved up and down, the wing becomes entirely separated from the body, leaving the imitation looking like anything but a minnow. Unfortunately, bodies of tapering floss just don't give the oval appearance that is desired.

All these considerations finally led me to discard the usual tying procedures. I began to look for new ways to tie a natural-looking artificial. The first problem I wanted to solve was the question of how to tie a realistic head. The idea I came up with was to tie a small bundle of brown bucktail to the top of the hook and let the tip ends extend straight forward over the hook eye, then match it with a small bundle of white bucktail tied in the same way *underneath* the hook. If the hair was anchored snugly behind the hook eye, then reversed and pulled back tightly towards the hook bend and held in this position with a slim collar of tying thread well back from the hook eye, a realistic head could be shaped. A uniform color scheme from nose to tail could also be achieved, and the oval body would be simulated by the body completely surrounding the hook shank. When the head was solidly coated with clear lacquer, a colored lacquer eye could be accurately positioned on it. One would have to be careful to keep the brown hair on top of the hook shank and the white hair beneath it, in order to provide a good color break through the head and body. The hair would have to be long enough to extend slightly beyond the hook bend after it has been reversed and tied back. The hook shank would be well buried under the bucktail, but to provide a bit of flash under the hair, silver tinsel could be wrapped the full length of the shank. A 6X-long hook seemed to be the most suitable size.

I kicked this idea around for a couple of years before sitting down and making one of the flies. In the spring of 1962, when planning a trip to northern Wisconsin, I decided to make a couple of brown and white bucktails according to this method and try them out. I also tied a version to which I added a lateral stripe of blue bucktail and another with an orchid lateral line. All were tied with silver tinsel on the hook shank. The brown and white fly was designed after the common shiner, or silver shiner, as it's also called. The one with the blue lateral line was meant to imitate a baitfish known as the straw-colored minnow, and the one with the orchid coloring was an attempt to imitate a smelt.

I soon came to realize that I was far too generous with material on these first few flies. I used about three times as much bucktail as was needed. The main thing, though, that bothered me about those first versions was the down-eye hooks I had used. The bending eye spoiled the elongated silhouette and gave the head a turtlelike look. The overdressing also contributed to this odd appearance. At any rate, I decided to try the flies out, so

22

packed them into my fishing vest and took them along on the Wisconsin trip.

When staying in the North Woods for any length of time, we always managed a trip to a fine little brook-trout stream called Thunder Creek. It's a typical small north-country stream flowing through swamps, woods, and meadows, finally joining a larger river. The water is cold spring water, tea-colored but pure, and the brookies thrive there. When I first became acquainted with Thunder Creek there was an ample flow all summer long, and the stream could only be reached by a long hike through the woods. These things have changed in recent years, and so have the size and number of trout, but Thunder Creek is still a challenging little brook to fish. There's another thing about Thunder Creek that I enjoy. It has a good-sized beaver dam, and although the dam is partially destroyed from time to time, it is always interesting to note its stage of construction and to fish the pool above.

When we arrived at Thunder Creek everything was pretty much as I had remembered it. Unless the trout were rising to floating flies, I always fished the creek with wets, usually starting out with either a Royal Coachman or a Grizzly King. On this particular day nothing was breaking the surface. I started out with my favorites and proceeded through my entire array of wet flies, but got very little action. Looking through my flybox for something to try next, I decided to tie on the little reversed-head brown and white bucktail. There were plenty of small minnows in the stream, and often when you thought you had engaged a trout, it would turn out to be what was locally known as a horned dace. The dace provided a good deal of forage for the trout, and the little bucktail worked very well. I wound up catching quite a few brook trout that day, several of respectable size, but I didn't try the bucktails with the colored lateral lines.

The next few days of vacation were nonfishing days, and during that time I thought about the reversed-head bucktails and what could be done to improve the turtlelike appearance of the heads. When you can't go fishing, the next best thing is to go down to a tackle shop and fondle fishing gear, so that's what I did. Besides, I wanted to ask some questions about where the hot spots were. At the store I discovered some long-shanked ringed-eye bait hooks, and I bought several dozen in different sizes. These ringed-eye hooks seemed perfectly suited to my purpose. On the way out, I had to explain to the shop owner, whom I knew well, what a fly fisherman was going to do with bait hooks. I'm not at all sure he bought my story.

Using the ring-eyed hooks, I tied a few more silver shiners, cutting down a great deal on the amount of bucktail used but otherwise following the same tying procedures as before. The result was a fly with much sleeker lines to the head. The hook eye seemed to blend in with the head lines and become part of the fly itself. I have since found that ringed-eye hooks do not balance in the water as well as down eyes, which put more weight under the hook and provide better keel, but the worst that can happen is that a ring-eyed fly will flip belly up once in a while. This can sometimes be an advantage. The turned-over fly takes on the appearance of an injured minnow and may bring on a strike that might not otherwise come your way. Usually, however, the tendency of a fly to turn over is an indication of overdressing, especially overdressing on the top part of the fly. If a fly turns over, the tier should go lighter on material on his next flies.

I tested the improved version on the Prairie River, a much larger stream than Thunder Creek. A minnow imitation could be worked really well on long casts here. The Prairie is mainly smooth flowing with deep, wide pools that harbor both brook and brown trout, the browns running to very good size. It develops a rich weed growth in the summer, not unlike some of our limestone streams. It also carries an abundance of baitfish. On a back-country dirt road we parked by a bridge that crossed the stream. Just above this bridge there was a beautiful pool that was too deep to be waded, but a long cast could reach the far bank where the cold waters of a large natural spring pond flowed into the river. I'll never forget the first cast I made that morning. It wasn't the size of the brownie that so much impressed me but rather the savage way he took the size-10 silver shiner. The fly landed near the bank on the far side of the stream, and I'd retrieved it only about five feet when he hit. He turned out to be just over two pounds, but he fought like a five-pounder and covered every corner of the pool in his efforts to rid himself of the little bucktail. It turned out to be a good day all the way around, and I came home with a great deal of fondness for the new reversed-head bucktails tied on ringed-eye hooks.

Back in New York State I set about convincing close fishing friends to try some of the new bucktails. I recall

25

being accused of scattering samples around like snow flakes in order to make sure that someone would catch a fish on one. One fellow angler told me that he didn't catch a single trout on the bucktail I gave him but he sure caught every yellow perch in the stream. He suggested that I name the new flies in honor of this most colorful species. That reminded me that there's no point in creating something new if you don't give it a name. Individual flies could be named after the baitfish they imitate, but the new dressing style itself had to be identified, so as to eliminate any possible confusion with flies bearing the same individual names but dressed in the conventional manner. I named the tying style after Thunder Creek, where the flies were first put to the test, and in honor of the beautiful, dark speckled trout that live in the waters of that typical northern Wisconsin trout stream.

3
How to Tie the Thunder Creek Series

have already talked about the general tying procedures to be followed in making the Thunder Creek bucktails. Now we'll look at each step in full detail. No special tools or materials are required, though I prefer a rotation vise to a stationary one because it allows me to easily look at all sides of the fly while I'm tying it. The new flat tying threads are also desirable, as they enable the tier to finish the fly off with a thin band of thread that doesn't destroy the sleek lines of the imitation. I use red thread because it often happens that a minnow's gill covers will show a flash of red as it is feeding or breathing or when it's frightened. I sometimes use the red thread just for finishing off and use a heavier, stronger white thread for the other tying operations. This is particularly helpful when you're tying on the tinsel, which sometimes severs the fine thread. (I prefer to use embossed tinsel to wrap the hook shank. It appears to give better flash in the water than the flat kind.)

Hook size depends on the size of the natural that one intends to imitate. It's a good idea to be familiar with the baitfish that are in the water you intend to fish. I have gone as large as 4/0 under extreme conditions, but I usually range my sizes from size 10s through size 2s. Although ringed-eye hooks work best, the bucktails can also be satisfactorily tied on down-eye hooks. If this is done, a small section of hook shank behind the eye—where the shank bends before the eye itself is formed—should be left bare of tying materials. If you do not leave this space, the head will look awkward and to some extent the sleek lines of your imitation will be spoiled.

There are seven basic steps for tying a bucktail in the Thunder Creek style when the pattern calls for a colored lateral stripe. If the pattern does not call for this lateral marking, step three is eliminated but all others remain the same. To illustrate the procedure, I have selected the Blacknose Dace, which calls for all seven of the tying steps. After finishing this fly you will be able to tie all of the Thunder Creek patterns. Each of the following stages of construction is accompanied by a photo showing what the fly should look like when that particular step is finished. Let's try one.

Place a size-8 6X-long ringed-eye hook in the vise, at- **1**
tach red tying thread behind the eye, and wrap the
thread solidly to the hook bend.

Tie in a piece of wide embossed silver tinsel at the bend
of the hook, then wrap the tying thread forward to the
head area. Wrap the tinsel forward so that it covers the **2**
hook shank solidly and tie it off a short distance behind
the hook eye. This operation should provide a very slim
line of flash. Bulk is undesirable.

Tie in a few black bucktail hairs in conventional down- **3**
wing style, leaving considerably more room than normal
in the head area. Clip off the butt ends of the hair and
wrap over them solidly with tying thread. The hair
should extend along the shank to just beyond the hook
bend, and the tip ends should be fairly even, with no
short hairs, or very few, mixed in.

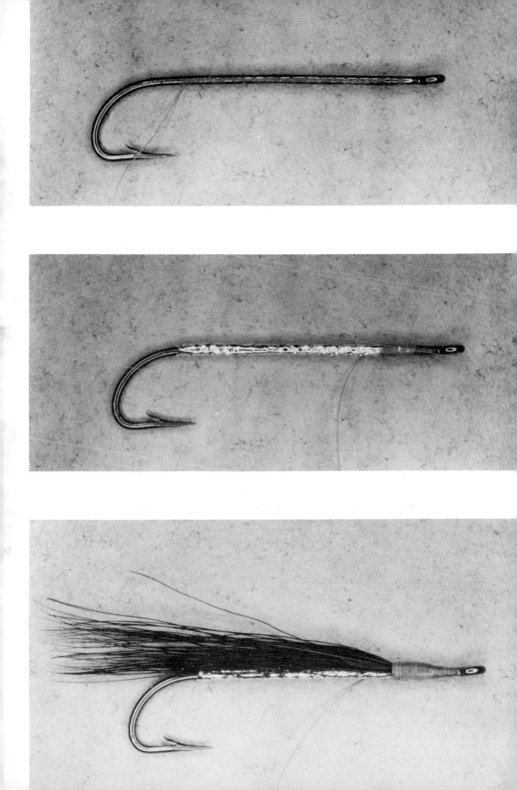

Attach a small bundle of brown bucktail hair on top of **4**
the hook so that the tip ends, which should be fairly even
and with no short hairs, extend forward over the hook
eye. In binding the hair down, continue the tying thread
forward right up tightly behind the hook eye and allow
the hair to spread out so that it covers the top 180
degrees of the hook shank. In other words, the hair
should spread completely across the top part of the
hook, but none of the fibers should be allowed to drop
toward the underside of the fly. You can check for
proper length of the hair by folding the tip ends back
toward the bend of the hook to see that when finally
affixed in the reverse position they will extend slightly
beyond the hook bend and will be of the same length as
the black hair. Then pull the brown hair back to its
forward position and trim off the butt ends and bind
down the stubs tightly. Place a drop of lacquer on the
wrappings at this point.

Turn the hook over in the vise and attach a small bundle **5**
of white bucktail hairs to the underside of the fly in the
same way that you attached the brown hair in the
preceding step. Allow the white hair to cover the bottom
180 degrees of the hook shank. The white hair should be
the same length as the brown hair, or slightly shorter.
This can easily be checked by forcing the brown and
white hairs together with your fingers. Trim off the butt
ends of the white hair and bind the stubs down tightly.
Another drop of lacquer should now be placed on the
bindings. Any unevenness in the head area where the
bucktail has been anchored can now be filled in with
extra turns of tying thread. These thread wrappings
should run smoothly from directly behind the hook eye
right back to where the head will end. This should cover
an area that is about one fifth the length of the entire fly.

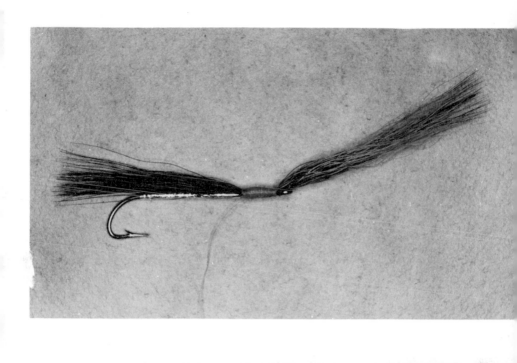

The fly should now be returned to its upright position in the vise and the brown and white hair reversed by pulling it back tightly along the hook shank toward the hook bend. Take care to keep the brown strands on the top 180 degrees of the shank and the white on the bottom 180 degrees of the shank. I usually make sure that the two sections are well separated before I reverse them. A small amount of tying wax on the fingers of the hand you use to reverse the hair will make it much easier to hold the hair tightly back against the head underwrappings. You may have to release the hair and repeat this reversing procedure several times before you are satisfied with the results. When the hair is properly reversed it will be snug against the head underwrappings and the brown and white strands will meet on each side of the fly head in a nice straight line, making a definite color break through the head and along the body of the imitation. The bucktail fibers should now completely surround the hook shank with the tying thread protruding through the bucktail fibers at the base of the head. While holding the hair in this reversed position, wrap the tying thread firmly around the hair at the back of the head, anchoring the hair permanently in the reversed position. These turns of thread should be very close together, so as to form a narrow red ring at the back of the head. This red ring will simulate the red flash of the open gill covers. Complete the tying process by whip finishing the thread.

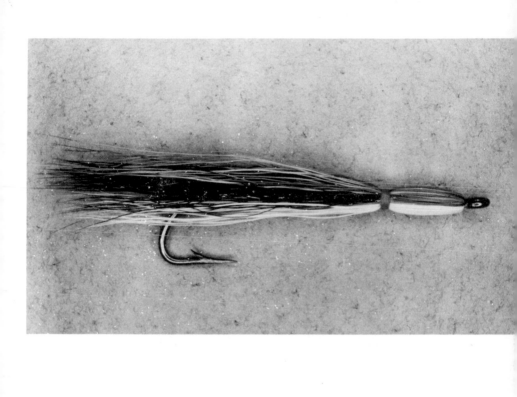

Bucktail hair will tend to spread out like a paintbrush as a result of the tying operation that affixes the strands in the reverse position. These strands can be forced down with the fingers. I usually moisten the hair when the preceding step is completed, then press it tightly around the hook shank and allow it to dry. This will control it from then on. At any rate, after the fly has been fished, the fibers will pull in closely together and hold their position well. After the fly has been moistened, give the entire head three coats of fairly heavy clear lacquer (water white preferred), allowing ample drying time between each coat. Paint an eye on the center of each side of the head by dabbing on a small drop of yellow lacquer and placing a smaller dot of black lacquer within the yellow dot. The head of a small finishing nail dipped in the lacquer and touched to the side of the fly head makes a neat eye. I have also used round cocktail toothpicks for this purpose. To really dress up the Blacknose Dace, draw a narrow black-lacquer line along the sides of the head from the hook eye to the base of the head, following the dividing line of the brown and white hair. This should be done before you apply the eye, which can then be centered on this line. These black head markings blend in with the black hair previously put on and create an imitation with the exact markings found on the natural minnow. When you remove the fly from the vise, arrange the belly hair so that it straddles the hook bend and point, which arrangement cannot be accurately made during the tying process, because the vise jaws are clamped on the hook bend. This provides for good balance and helps hide the hook.

7

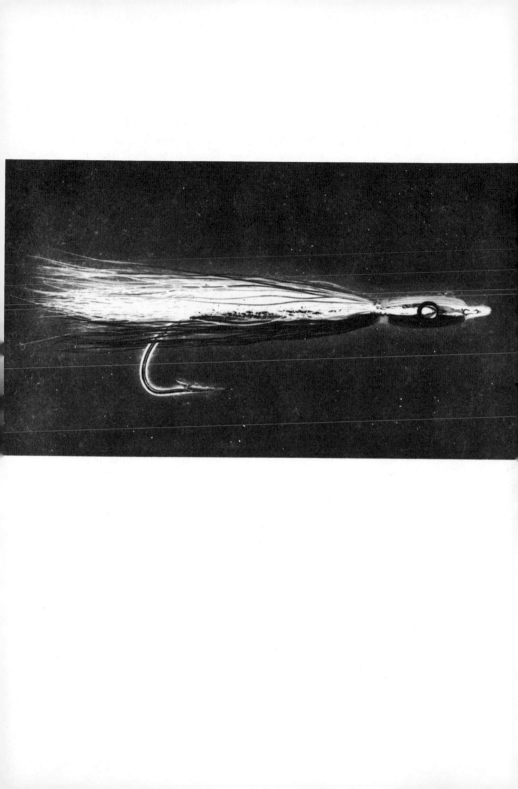

I selected bucktail hair as the material for the Thunder Creek flies because of its general qualities. I prefer to use the hair on the bottom half of the tail because it is a little coarser and straighter than the strands of the tip section. Very few hairs need be used on a fly because when they are reversed the hair in the head area flattens out and covers the under wrappings very well. This function of the hair allows a fly to be tied very sparsely, and sparseness is much to be desired. I have always found that a lightly dressed bucktail will stir up more strikes and take more fish than an overdressed one. If you think you have made your fly too sparse and have lost the lateral coloring of the fly, just hold it up.to the light and you'll be surprised at how strongly the color comes through. This brilliancy is one of the great qualities of bucktail. It also soaks up water well, which gives it a smooth, minnowlike appearance. Besides all of these things, bucktail is quite durable and will give good service. Further, it is easily available, inexpensive, and can be dyed to any color. I have tried a good many types of hair as substitutes for bucktail, but none can match its qualities for making the Thunder Creek series.

Except for the Marabou Shiner, each pattern in the series calls for bucktail and follows the procedure we have just covered. Because of the nature of marabou, a little special treatment must be given to it. The mechanics for steps 4 and 5 are the same as described, but in step 4 you use a silver-pheasant crest feather in place of bucktail, and in step 5 you use the top part of a single white marabou feather with the very tip clipped out, which gives it a "V" appearance. In step 6 the reversing technique varies slightly. Instead of reversing both the back and belly parts together, fold back the white marabou first and anchor it with several turns of thread. I let the fibers come up over the halfway point on the sides of the head, since the back material can be adjusted to give the break in the color scheme. I sometimes put a touch of white lacquer on the bottom part of the thread wrappings before reversing the white marabou, as this helps to hold the white color of the throat. If this is not done, you will sometimes get a flash of the red tying thread showing through in the throat area. This use of white lacquer is not necessary on bucktail patterns. After reversing the white marabou, fold the silver-pheasant crest feather back and finish the fly. In so doing, you can adjust this feather to give a good straight line along each side of the head. Now give the head the usual three coats of clear lacquer. Applying the first coat, allow the lacquer to become good and tacky, then gently rub your finger over the head of the fly toward the bend of the hook. This will cause all of the little flues to lie down and adhere to each other. Allow the head to dry thoroughly before applying the next two coats of lacquer. Center the eyes on the head, and the fly is finished.

Although I rarely fish with a weighted fly, there are times when a little lead can mean the difference between action and no action. Any of the Thunder Creek patterns can be weighted by wrapping lead wire or a piece of strip lead around the hook shank before the tying process is started. When lead is applied, I wrap over it solidly with tying thread before going on with the second step. This permanently anchors the lead, so that it will not twist around the hook shank and loosen the body.

39

4

The Thunder Creek Patterns and Their Living Counterparts

In my opinion, coloring is very important in creating a baitfish imitation but not as vitally important as shape and general appearance. Some species of baitfish are distinctly different from others in their coloring, though many species have similar shadings and markings. On the other hand, all these fish have slim, elongated oval shapes and dominant heads and eyes. As a result, a fly patterned after a specific baitfish can prove very successful in water where that particular species doesn't exist. Yet trout can be almost as selective to baitfish as they often are to floating duns, and that's why the exact color combination is important.

In working toward developing a series of patterns that would cover most fishing situations, I tried many color combinations in attempting to copy a number of prominent baitfish. I finally settled on trying to reproduce the dominant colors rather than attempting to work in each little shading variation. I eventually developed seven patterns that copied seven different baitfish. I also worked up a pattern for the Mickey Finn, for no reason other than that its color arrangement was right for the new style of tying, though I soon dropped this red and yellow fly, as I wanted to limit the patterns to imitations of living counterparts. Later, I slightly rearranged a few of the original patterns, renamed one, and gradually added new imitations until presently there are fifteen flies in the series.

The fifteen flies all differ somewhat from each other in color combinations, but all have the same general appearance. All but one are designed after a specific fish. This exception, the Marabou Shiner, is a general-purpose fly that I often use as a "locater" pattern. The magic of marabou is something that a bucktail or streamer fisherman should never be without. I think often of the fifteen flies as primary patterns and the remaining five as secondary patterns. The reason for this is that the ten primaries offer a generally satisfactory range of color assortments and are designed after the more common and broadly distributed baitfish. The secondaries are designed after baitfish that are restricted in their distribution or in the type of water they inhabit. These flies are not as useful as the primaries.

There is hardly a limit to the number of patterns that could be added to the series or to the color arrangements that can be attempted. The tying style lends itself to imitating almost any small fish reasonably well. All it takes is imagination and a good selection of bucktails in a variety of colors.

In the following pages I have listed each of the fifteen patterns, giving detailed information on the materials that go into their construction. I have also given brief descriptions of the fish that the flies are designed after. There is considerable confusion in the scientific classification of fish, especially when it comes to the shiners and darters, but I have tried to be specific and accurate in my names and descriptions. It should be remembered, though, that reclassification is constantly taking place and common names often vary in different locations.

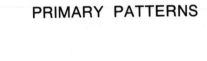

PRIMARY PATTERNS

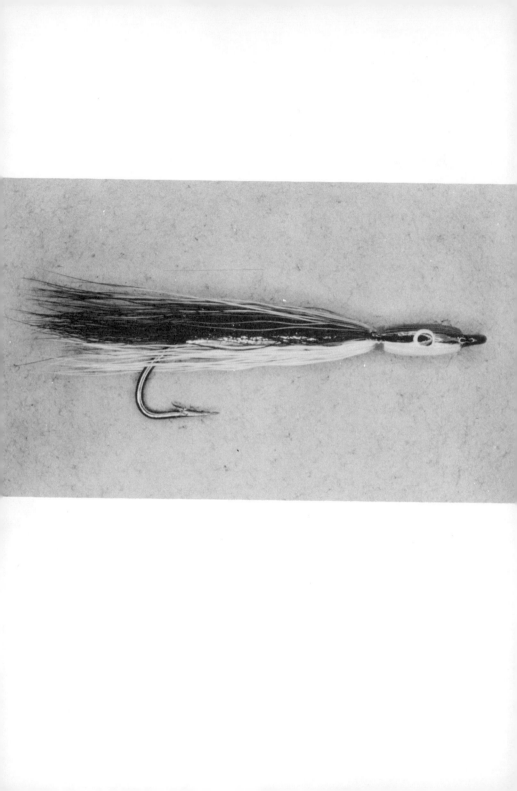

Blacknose Dace *(Rhinichthys atratulus)*

This minnow inhabitants small, clear brooks and streams and prefers moving water to motionless pools. It is a fairly hardy fish and has a good range extending across the northern half of the U.S. from the East Coast through the Midwest and up into Canada. It gets its name from its blackish nose and the black lateral stripe that runs along the center of its body from the tip of its nose to its tail. This stripe, or band, as it is sometimes called, passes through the center of the minnow's eye, and the pupil of the eye itself seems to be part of the color scheme. The color of the back can vary from shades of brown or olive brown to almost black. The belly is white or cream colored. It's a graceful little fish, and a few crumbs of bread dropped in a school of them can be very entertaining. The average length of the minnow is not much more than a couple of inches. There are quite a few other species of minnows with similar dark lateral stripes, so a good imitation of the blacknose dace can cover a lot of ground.

This pattern is tied on hooks ranging from size 10 through size 2, but hooks on the larger end of this range are seldom called for. The hook shank covering is silver embossed tinsel. The lateral stripe is a small bundle of black bucktail hair. The top of the head and the back are made from natural brown bucktail; the bottom of the head and the belly are made from white bucktail. After the head is well coated with clear lacquer, a black lacquer line is drawn on each side of the head from the hook eye to the base of the head, following the dividing line of the brown and white hair. Use a very fine artist's brush for this purpose. The yellow lacquer eye with a black lacquer pupil should be centered on the head.

Emerald Shiner *(Notropis atherinoides)*

These shiners have a broad range in the U.S. and Canada and are primarily found in large clear-water lakes, although they sometimes run into streams. They get their name from a typical faintly marked emerald-green lateral strip. The top of the head and the back of the fish are a light to medium shade of brown. Its underparts are white. It is an excellent forage fish for trout, landlocked salmon, and other game species. The emerald shiner is quite small, averaging about three inches in length. Except for its size, it has much the same slim appearance as the smelt.

This fly is tied on hooks from size 10 through size 2. The hook-shank covering is embossed green tinsel or fluorescent green floss ribbed with medium-width embossed silver tinsel. This will show through the bucktail as a lateral stripe. The top of the head and back are made from brown bucktail; the bottom of the head and belly are white bucktail. The eye is yellow lacquer with a black lacquer dot.

Golden Shiner *(Notemigonus crysoleucas)*

These baitfish generally travel in large schools and mainly inhabit ponds, lakes, and very slow streams. Although they are primarily a warm-water fish, I have found them in considerable numbers in lakes where the game fish are predominantly trout. The golden shiner can run up to eight inches or better. They are found over a wide area from Canada to Mexico. Their name comes from the golden coloring of their deep flat sides. One of their characteristics is to cruise close to the surface of a lake, allowing their backs and dorsal fins to just break the water. They can provide good sport on a small wet fly when they are on the top, but when you see them scatter you know that a large game fish is raising havoc with them. The backs of these fish range from a brown in the smaller sizes to greenish brown or bluish green in more mature specimens. Their bellies are whitish.

This fly is tied on hooks ranging from size 6 through size 4/0, and I have also tied them on a tandem setup, using heavy gold mylar piping with the core removed to connect the hooks. On single hooks the hook-shank covering is embossed yellow tinsel. The lateral stripe is a small bundle of bright yellow dyed bucktail. The top of the head and the back are made from brown bucktail or the brown part of a dyed green or blue bucktail. The bottom of the head and the belly consist of white bucktail strands. The eye is yellow lacquer with a black-lacquer pupil.

49

Marabou Shiner

There is no actual minnow called the Marabou Shiner, and the fly listed below is not designed after a specific baitfish. It was created to provide a general pattern for the broad category of minnows that have dark backs and white underparts with sides of a bright silvery cast. I have found this marabou fly to provide a very good second pattern for the common shiner. It's a good pattern for blind fishing. There is probably no material for baitfish imitations that provides better, more natural action in the water than marabou feathers. It's always a good idea to carry a marabou streamer and to use it when the going gets tough or when you are fishing in unfamiliar waters. You will be surprised at how fast you can find out where the fish are.

This pattern can be tied in a full range of hook sizes from size 10 on up. The hook-shank covering is embossed silver tinsel. The top of the head and the back are made from a single silver pheasant crest feather, just the way it comes off the bird. The bottom of the head and the belly are made from the top section of a white marabou plume with the tip part clipped out. The idea is to remove the center quill of the feather so that it won't interfere with the action of the marabou fibers. The eye is yellow lacquer with a black lacquer dot. If you find silver-pheasant crest feathers hard to come by, you can substitute the tip section of a marabou plume dyed black for the top part of the fly. Special instructions for making this fly are given in Chapter 3.

51

Rainbow Trout *(Salmo gairdneri)*

This great game fish is so well known in its different varieties and by its wide distribution that it seems unnecessary to give even a brief comment about it. It is the greatest of all game fish in my estimation. Our interest in it here comes from the fact that the rainbow is a stream spawner, and although it typically migrates to the ocean or to large lakes as it matures, it spends its youth in fresh-water streams where it is vulnerable to various types of predators, including larger game fish. Its name is derived from the bright pink lateral stripe that adorns its sides. Its back is a medium shade of green and the underparts are white. The rainbow is usually covered with small black spots, but many of the immature fish and migratory specimens just returned to the stream from larger bodies of water have a silvery tone with fewer spots. In streams, the rainbow has a fondness for the fastest water and can sometimes be seen leaping for natural insects right in the white water.

This fly is made on hook sizes ranging from size 10 through size 2 and even larger if you prefer. The hook shank covering is embossed silver tinsel. The lateral stripe is white bucktail dyed a strong, true pink. The top of the head and the back of the fly are made from hair of the brown part of a bucktail dyed green. The bottom of the head and the belly are made from white bucktail strands. The eye is yellow lacquer with a black lacquer pupil.

53

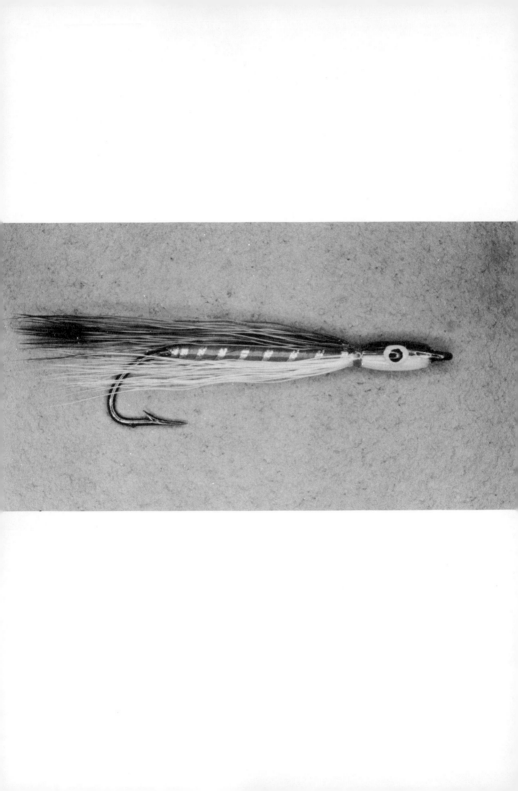

Redfin Shiner *(Notropis cornutus)*

The redfin, which is actually the adult male of the common shiner species, gets its name from the fact that its fins and the lower part of its sides take on a brilliant red hue during the spawning run. Its back is generally a brownish olive, and its belly is white with a brushing of pink or red. From the side it looks silvery, but a few of the scales have a dark shading that gives the minnow a somewhat mottled appearance. The redfin is a large baitfish, growing to eight inches or better. It's distribution is very wide. It inhabits fast-moving streams and provides good forage for trout and other game fish. There is another shiner with a different scientific name that is also called the redfin shiner. This minnow is a good deal smaller than the common shiner, and does not have as wide a distribution, so it's not as popular a baitfish as the common shiner. (More information on the common shiner is given in the description of the silver shiner.)

This fly is tied on hook sizes ranging from 10 through 4/0. The hook shank covering is deep pink or red fluorescent floss ribbed with medium-width embossed silver tinsel. The top of the head and the back are made from brown bucktail; the bottom of the head and the belly are white bucktail. The eye is yellow lacquer with a black lacquer dot.

55

Silver Shiner *(Notropis cornutus)*

The common shiner species of baitfish is known by many names and one of these names is the silver shiner. This minnow is found throughout North America. It inhabits rapidly moving streams as well as lakes and ponds that have inlet streams providing satisfactory spawning places. The male of this species, which takes on a red hue at spawning time, is known as the redfin shiner. It is described above under that heading. The female and immature fish of the common-shiner species are plain silvery minnows with a slight mottling of dark scales scattered along their sides. Their backs are brownish olive, the stomachs are white. The females are not as large as the males, which reach a length of eight inches or more. Because of their generous distribution and the fact that they live in fast-water streams, silver shiners provide good larder for trout and other game fish. There is at least one other species of shiner called the silver shiner. It is smaller and differs somewhat in appearance from the common shiner and, of course, has a different scientific name. It does not have the wide distribution or the popularity of the common shiner.

This fly is tied on hooks ranging from size 10 to much larger sizes. The hook shank covering is embossed silver tinsel. The top of the head and the back are made from brown bucktail; the bottom of the head and the belly are white bucktail. I usually make these flies with backs in different shades of brown, from dark to light, to provide a good range of colors. The eyes are yellow lacquer with black lacquer pupils. The silver shiner is the simplest pattern in the series, and the materials it calls for are very easy to obtain, yet it has proved to be one of the most productive flies in the series. It can also be made in tandem-hook form, using heavy silver mylar piping with the core removed to connect the hooks. This method provides extremely good flash.

57

Smelt *(Osmerus mordax)*

There are a number of smelt species, all quite similar in shape and coloring, but the one of prime interest to the sportsman angler is the American, or Atlantic, smelt. This species is anadromous and was originally found along the northeastern Atlantic seaboard of the U.S. and on up into Canadian waters. Through numerous plantings, it now also exists in a landlocked form in many cold-water lakes of the northeastern U.S. and Canada, as well as in the Great Lakes. It is an especially good baitfish for trout and landlocked salmon. It is a slim, silvery fish that reaches a maximum length of about fourteen inches but averages about half that size. It has a large head with big teeth. Its back coloring varies on individual fish from light tan to dark olive. The sides are silvery with a tint of orchid coloring, and its under parts are a silvery white. Most of the other species of smelt originate in the Pacific, and of those, one commonly known as the candlefish is the most important. It too is an anadromous species and enters many of the great salmon and steelhead streams of western Canada and the northwestern U.S.

This fly is tied on a range of hook sizes, from 6 to much larger sizes. The hook shank covering is embossed silver tinsel. The lateral stripe is white bucktail dyed orchid color. The top of the head and the back are brown bucktail; the bottom of the head and the belly are white bucktail. The eye is yellow lacquer with a black lacquer pupil.

59

Spottail Shiner *(Notropis hudsonius)*

This shiner mainly inhabits large rivers and lakes, although it enters feeder streams to spawn. It has a broad range across Canada and the northern half of the U.S., from the East coast to the Rocky Mountains. It travels in schools and gets its name from a very distinct black caudal spot, which is centered just in front of the tail on both sides of its body. Its back is an olive color that sometimes takes on an iridescence with shadings of green and purple. It tends to have a lateral stripe that can be suggested by gold tinsel; its underparts are white. A small minnow of three to four inches, the spottail is an important food source for game fish.

This fly is tied on hook sizes ranging from 10s through 2s. A very short piece of heavy black floss cut off flat is tied in at the bend of the hook to simulate the caudal spot that gives this minnow its name. The hook shank covering is embossed gold tinsel. The top part of the head and the back are made from hair of the brown part of a green-dyed bucktail; the bottom of the head and the belly are white bucktail. The eye is yellow lacquer with a black lacquer dot.

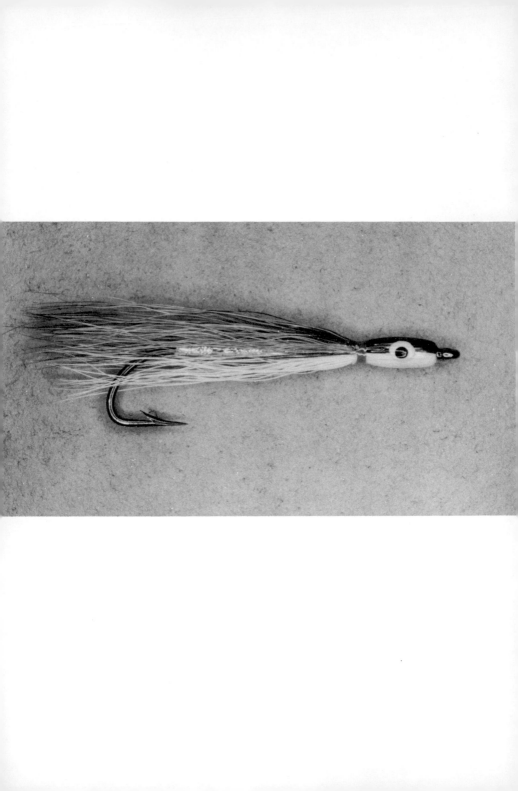

Strawcolor Shiner *(Notropis stramineus)*

This shiner, also known as the sand shiner, is primarily found along the sandy beaches of large rivers and lakes. It is not distributed over as broad an area as the other baitfish in the primary-pattern category. However, its general coloring is similar to that of many other small baitfish, and for that reason I've included it in this section. Its name no doubt comes from the tints of blues and pinks that can be seen in straw when it is closely examined, because this shiner has similar shadings. Its back is a dark rosy brown that lightens in the caudal region to a strong pink. Its sides are of a bluish tint, its underparts are white. The strawcolor shiner grows to not much more than three inches in length.

Hook sizes from 10 through 2 cover the size range of this baitfish. The hook shank covering is embossed silver tinsel. The lateral stripe is made from a few hairs from the white part of a bucktail dyed medium blue. The top of the head and the back are made from the brown part of a bucktail dyed a strong, true pink. The bottom of the head and the belly are white bucktail. The eye is yellow lacquer with a black lacquer pupil.

63

Blacknose Dace

Blacknose
Dace

Emerald
Shiner

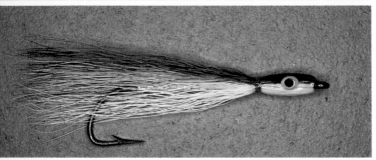

Golden
Shiner

Marabou
Shiner

Rainbow
Trout

PATTERNS

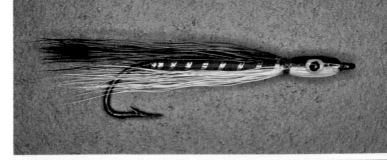

*Redfin
Shiner*

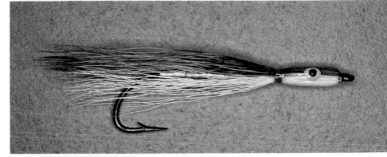

*Silver
Shiner*

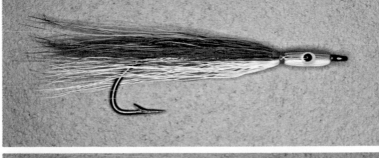

Smelt

*Spottail
Shiner*

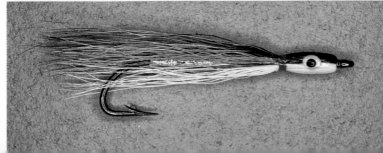

*Strawcolor
Shiner*

Redlip Shiner

Steelcolor Shiner

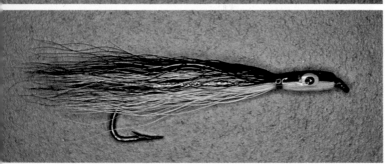

Striped Jumprock

Swamp Darter

Wedgespot Shiner

SECONDARY PATTERNS

Redlip Shiner   *(Notropis chiliticus)*

This small shiner reaches only a couple of inches in length and has a very limited distribution, being found only in Virginia and South Carolina. The male of the species has a pale yellow or olive cast with a black lateral stripe and a black dorsal surface. Its dorsal and anal fins are of fairly good size and are bright orange to red. It has a green shading around the eyes, and the tip of its nose and lips are bright red. The females are less bright and are generally more silvery.

Hook sizes from 10 through 4 are suggested. A piece of black floss is tied in at the bend of the hook and cut off flat and fairly short to act as an extention of the black lateral stripe. The hook shank covering is a thin layer of black floss. This floss is used during the wrapping process to tie in two pieces of burnt-orange floss, one on the bottom of the hook a third of the way in from the bend, to represent the anal fin, and the other on top of the hook half way in from the bend, to represent the dorsal fin. These orange-floss sections should be cut off to about a quarter inch in length. The finished hook shank covering is then ribbed with medium-width embossed gold tinsel. The hook-shank covering provides the lateral stripe on this fly, but a few bucktail hairs dyed a pale yellow are nevertheless placed in the usual lateral area to provide some color between the lateral stripe and the back of the imitation. The top of the head and the back are made from black dyed bucktail; the bottom of the head and the belly are pale yellow bucktail. After the head is well lacquered with clear lacquer, the top part of the head is mottled with pale-green lacquer and a bright red lacquer nose is added. A yellow lacquer eye with a black pupil is then centered on each side of the head.

66

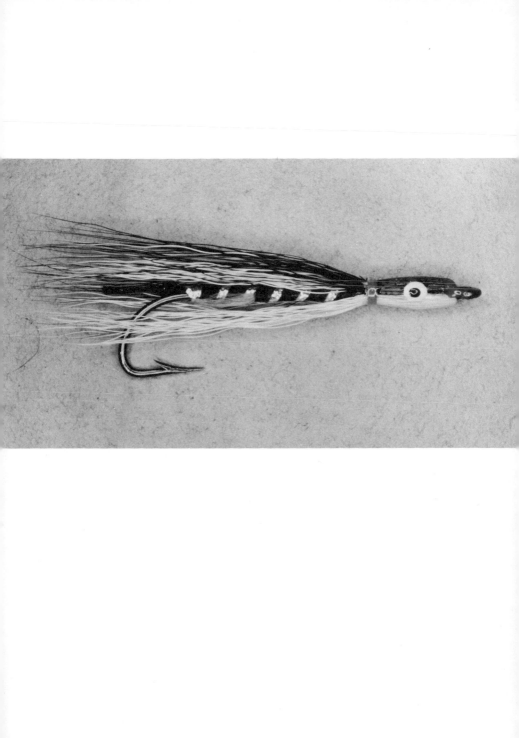

Steelcolor Shiner *(Notropis whipplei)*

This shiner is thought to be limited in range to a couple of midwestern states, but because of its similarity to other species its full range is probably unknown. It is often confused with the spotfin shiner and the satinfin shiner, both of which have a much broader range but are of about the same size. The dusky spot on the rear section of the dorsal fin no doubt causes confusion with the spotfin, which has the same marking, while the faint yellow coloring on the fins of breeding males is probably the reason it is confused with the satinfin. The steelcolor shiner is a silvery fish with a bluish-brown back. It has a steel-blue coloring through its lateral area, and its underparts are light cream, except for the breeding males, as noted above. It is basically a stream shiner of about four inches in length and provides good forage for game fish.

This fly is tied on hooks from size 10 through size 2. The hook shank covering is blue fluorescent floss with a medium-width embossed silver tinsel rib. The top of the head and the back are made from brown bucktail dyed blue. The bottom of the head and the belly are made from white bucktail dyed pale yellow. The eye is yellow lacquer with a black lacquer dot.

Striped Jumprock *(Moxostoma rupiscartes)*

This fish is one of the smaller species in the sucker family and has the typical underslung sucker mouth with protruding lips which enable it to feed from river bottoms. Its range is from North Carolina southward. It has a cousin, the Black Jumprock, that is quite similar in appearance. Both fish apparently get their names from their tendency to periodically leap clear of the water. The striped jumprock has a dark brown to almost black back, and its sides and underparts, including fins, are lighter with a shading of pink or pale orange. Several rows of dark scales along the upper part of its sides give it a striped appearance. Game fish enjoy dining on this small sucker.

This fly is tied on hooks ranging from size 6 to larger sizes. The hook shank covering is embossed gold tinsel. The lateral stripe is a very few hairs of white bucktail dyed pale orange. The top of the head and the back are made from very dark brown bucktail or the natural black hair that is sometimes found at the tip end of a bucktail. The bottom of the head and the belly are made from the same pale orange bucktail that is used for the lateral stripe. I find that white bucktail dyed pale orange takes on a very satisfactory pink cast, but pale pink dyed bucktail is also good. The eye is yellow lacquer with a black lacquer dot. I often tie this fly on a down-eye hook because the turned-down eye simulates the protruding lips of the sucker.

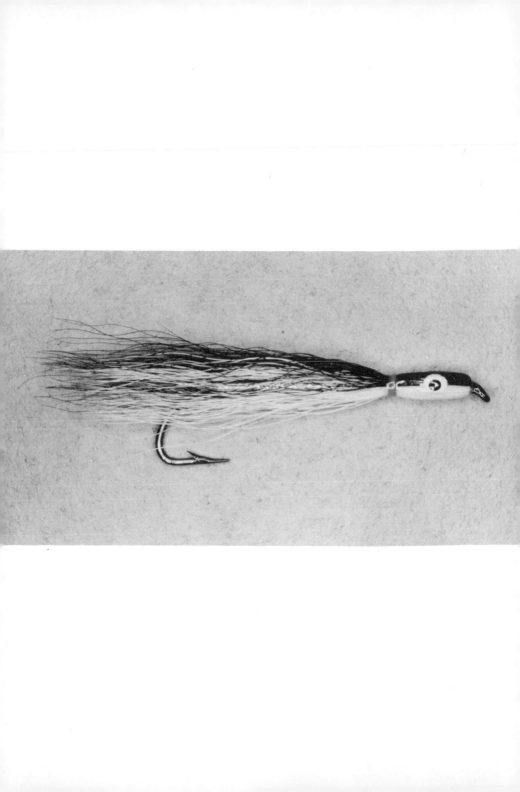

Swamp Darter *(Etheostoma fusiforme)*

The swamp darter, together with a very similar subspecies, had a broad range, running from the eastern seaboard as far west as Texas. These little bottom dwellers reach a maximum length of about three inches and derive their name from the swampy, gloomy waters that they inhabit. Like other species of darters they propel themselves along the bottom in rapid sporadic thrusts. Swamp darters have a dark blotchy appearance on their sides, with a general brownish-olive coloring throughout. Their underparts are in lighter tones suggestive of light tans or whites. Several other species of darters that live in clearwater streams, rivers, and lakes have a similar appearance to the swamp darters.

This is the only fly in the series that requires the use of hackle feathers in its construction, but it is basically a bucktail. It is tied on hooks ranging from size 10 through size 4. The hook-shank covering is embossed silver tinsel. The blotchy side markings are provided by tying in two very narrow grizzly saddle hackles back to back in conventional down-wing style. The top of the head and the back are made from medium-brown bucktail. The bottom of the head and the belly are white bucktail. The eye is yellow lacquer with a black lacquer dot and is placed well forward on the head. This fly should have a very slim appearance.

72

Wedgespot Shiner *(Notropis greenei)*

This shiner has a very limited distribution, being found only in certain rivers in several central and southcentral states, but bass are very fond of it. Reaching a length of not more than three inches, the wedgespot gets its name from a dark triangular or wedge-shaped caudal spot. Its back has a light to medium olive cast, and the underparts are light cream color or white. It carries a brownish lateral stripe with a faint, fine black lateral line that follows along underneath and ties in with the caudal spot. The eye of this minnow is exceptionally large. The wedgespot looks somewhat like the spottail shiner and several other species with similar caudal markings.

This fly is tied on hooks ranging from size 10 through size 4. A piece of black floss is tied in at the bend of the hook and cut off very short to simulate the caudal spot. The hook shank is covered with a thin layer of black floss which is then ribbed closely with fine embossed silver tinsel. The lateral stripe is made by tying in two strands of brown floss which should extend back over the hook shank to the point where the caudal spot begins. The top of the head and the back are made from natural light-brown bucktail hair. The bottom of the head and the belly are of white bucktail. The eye is yellow lacquer with a black lacquer dot and should be painted extra large.

74

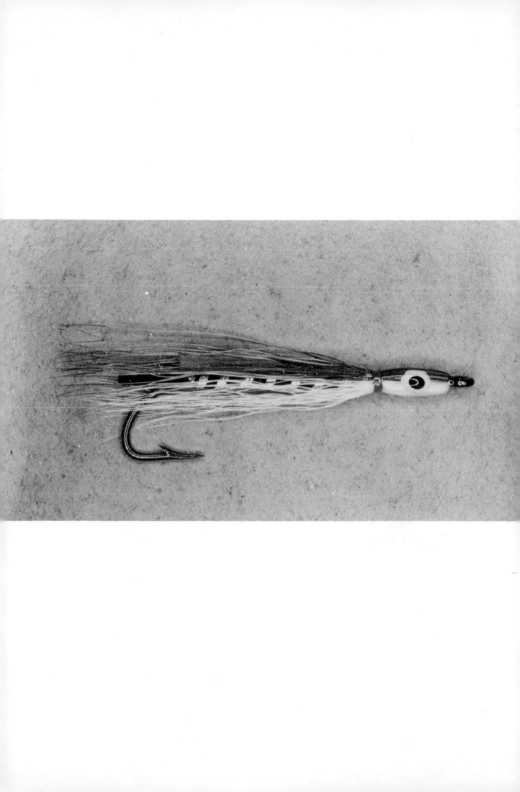

5
Reasons for Using Baitfish Imitations and Some Tackle Considerations

Bucktail and streamer fishing is surely the most neglected of all of fresh-water fly-fishing techniques. The main reason for this unfortunate situation appears to be tradition, which dictates that baitfish imitations are suited for use only in the high, cold waters of spring floods or at other times when streams are high or dirty. This feeling even carries over to lake fishing, where the long flies get their greatest use just after ice out or when the new season opens. Then, too, there's the feeling that bucktail and streamer fishing is on a low rung of the fly-fishing ladder. In any case, once the insect hatches come into their own, the long flies are laid aside until the hatches disappear. But actually, baitfish imitations provide excellent sport at any time of the season and, on the average, produce larger fish and are generally more useful under a wider variety of stream sizes and conditions than any other type of fly-rod lure. To try to es-

77

tablish this fact more firmly, let's take a look at some of the grounds for using a baitfish imitation.

You can hardly go wrong in selecting a baitfish imitation if you want to simulate a natural and very substantial food item that all game fish will readily take. Almost every body of water that contains game fish will also have some small fish in it. These little fellows may be the normal baitfish species or the young of various other types of fish, including those of the young of the game fish you are seeking, or very likely a combination of these. Matching an item in a sport fish's diet is what fishing with exact imitations is all about. However, fish will seemingly hit an imitation out of mere annoyance or perhaps out of inquisitiveness, and both of these situations can be covered very nicely with a baitfish imitation. You can take much better advantage of these last two situations if you can see the fish you are after, and it can be very interesting to watch the action. I remember once having a fifteen-inch brown trout follow a Spottail Shiner imitation right up to my boots several times. Each time he would go back to the center of the small stream I was fishing. Finally, I cast the fly out in front of him and let it sink to the bottom in the slow-moving water, where it lay motionless. The antics that followed were very odd, and I laughed out loud watching that fish. He would sidle up to the fly and look at it, but he sensed that something was wrong and would back off and circle the unmoving fly. Three times he darted in and tried to grab it and move out fast, but each time he missed and once flipped out of the water in his hurry to get away. He was like someone testing an iron to see if it's hot—you touch it with a wet finger but just fleetingly,

78

to avoid getting burned. Finally, his inquisitiveness got the best of him and he roared in, grabbed the bucktail, and was hooked. Then he took off in all directions at once. Needless to say, I returned him unharmed to his stream. After the show he'd put on I couldn't do otherwise.

It's great sport when you can see your game and guess at his emotions as you try out all your tricks, but most of the fishing with baitfish imitations is blind fishing, which brings us back to the importance of closely simulating a natural baitfish. The tendency of game fish to feed on smaller fish develops very early. I recall having an opportunity some years ago of watching a few fingerlings of various species under controlled conditions. None of the specimens was longer than two inches, and they averaged out to somewhere around an inch and a half. Gradually, over succeeding days, their numbers decreased until one day our suspicions were confirmed. The larger ones were consuming the smaller ones, and believe me they had a hard time doing it, but none the less the act was accomplished and the survivors grew rapidly. Game fish have phenomenally voracious appetites, and the way to take advantage of their gluttony is to offer them a baitfish imitation that looks and acts alive.

Fly fishermen generally agree that the most thrilling part of the sport is the strike and first run of a good fish, and many times, especially with trout, these two actions seem inseparable. There is no harder strike on any type of fly than the one that comes to a moving baitfish imitation. Consider that the game fish is chasing the fly and is moving at a good rate of speed when he hits it. If he is moving to intercept the fly, he must be traveling with a good head of steam to overtake the normal darting movements of a baitfish. Then, too, the strike has to be hard enough to stun and capture a live minnow. When the steel is driven home, the fish's flight is usually instantaneous because he already has a good start. When one is fishing with dry flies, wet flies, or nymphs the fly normally drifts in toward the fish, and his movements as he engulfs the fly are less strenuous, and even though he may get off to a fast start on his run, it won't quite come up to the rush he'd have in taking a moving bucktail.

I don't mean to imply that fishing with baitfish imitations is the only way to fish—far from it. Unless a fly fisherman uses all the different types of flies, he is not enjoying the sport to the fullest, because each type, whether it be dry, wet, nymph, or baitfish imitation, provides its own special pleasures, and there will be times when each one will be successful when all others fail. What I am suggesting is that fishing with baitfish imitations should not be ignored or left to only the early part of the season but should be put to general use throughout the year in all water conditions.

The choice of the right tackle for fishing a Thunder Creek fly, or for any other bucktail or streamer, is very important, especially in the matter of rod choice. Your control of the fly depends on your equipment as well as how you handle it. And the right gear will make your day more relaxing and pleasurable. In stream fishing, one of the first things to consider in selecting a rod for a particular outing is the size of the stream you are going to fish. The next thing is the stream conditions—is the water high, low, or in average flow? Is the area you are going to fish fast, slow, or of average speed? The answer to these questions will help you choose a rod best suited to the job at hand. For instance, if a small stream is high and fast or if you are fishing a larger river where deep wading and long casts are required, a rod in the seven-and-a-half to eight-foot range will do better work than a shorter one because it will give you more control over your line, and in the heavier, bigger water you need as much control as you can get. When standing waist deep in the water, you will be better able to keep your back casts up, thereby allowing longer and more accurate deliveries of the fly. But on small moderate flowing streams, or even big water that is low, there is no need to carry the extra weight of a long rod. A lighter and shorter one will allow you to cover the water just as well and more comfortably. Light, full-action rods are my favorites, and I always use the lightest one I have that will do the job at hand. Generally, I stick with a six- to seven-footer of no more than two and a half ounces for small- and medium-sized streams and a seven-and-a-half- to eight-footer for larger rivers. In lakes and the largest rivers I sometimes go to an eight-and-a-half-foot rod. Four ounces is about the top weight for this length. I prefer sliding-band reel seats for rods of seven feet or less and screw-locking seats on the longer ones.

Although I certainly have nothing against fine bamboo rods, and often use them, I long ago decided that top quality, hollow fiber-glass rods are the finest available at any price, and the lightest and strongest at a given rod length. A properly tapered glass rod with a smooth, easy action flowing right down into the grip will cast the proper weight line a country mile, and if the angler lets the rod do the work instead of his arm, and learns the rhythm of his rod, the job will come easy. The trouble is that too many glass rods are designed in an attempt to simulate bamboo action and are sold on this basis, instead of being made to bring out the fine qualities of fiber glass. The best rods I have ever used or seen are the hollow-glass masterpieces custom made by Vince Cummings of Dobbs Ferry, New York. Each one has the top quality workmanship that goes into the most expensive bamboos, but that's where the similarity ends. They range from a six-foot one-piece wand weighing a mere one ounce to a nine-footer of only four and a quarter ounces in two-piece construction, and they handle lines from number 4 on the lightest rods to number 8 on the big job. Vince's rods are superb in all respects.

As for reels, a sturdy light-weight single action is best. The reel should balance your rod near the front cork ring of the hand grip and provide adequate room for backing in addition to the fly line. It should run smoothly both forward and backward and allow for drag adjustment, although a reel with a one-position drag is satisfactory for small-stream fishing. It should also have provisions for quick take down, should you need to check its mechanical functioning at stream side or want to change spools. In addition, it should be convertible to left- or right-hand cranking. Any good reel should be able to take a certain amount of rough treatment and most certainly should stand up under the heated run of a good fish.

In streams of moderate depth, a floating line is preferable to one that sinks in its entirety or one with a sinking tip or sinking head. A floater is much easier to handle on retrieves and pick ups, is less tiring to use, and doesn't put as much strain on your rod. It also helps you work your bucktail more naturally, and this is especially true when you cast upstream and allow the fly to "swim" its way down through the current. As you gather in slack to keep pace with the speed of the flow and stay in touch with your lure, the serpentine movements of a floating line give the imitation a very effective action. And long casts across currents of varying speeds will result in a bellying of the line that will spoil the movement of the fly. If the line is beneath the water, it is just about inpossible to mend your line to correct this situation. But with a floater, a twitch of the rod in the direction opposite to the belly allows you to easily toss the line upstream, so that the fly can resume a natural drift. In moving water, sinking lines of all types tend to be swept aside by the current and will pile up in the quieter water at the edge of the flow. This will make pick-ups difficult and allow only short, unsatisfactory drifts of the fly. To get a bucktail down to a moderate depth, I much prefer to use a floating line and cast the fly upstream or into the current at such an angle that the weight of the hook will take the fly down before the retrieve is started. Many times a fish will take the fly as it sinks and the current is moving it along with plenty of action and causing it to look alive and natural. Weighting the fly is also a good way of scratching the bottom without the use of a sinking line, although a weighted fly is more difficult to cast than one with no lead and will loose some of the natural action the current gives an unweighted fly. On the other hand, for deep streams the sinker, with its drawbacks, is the best means of putting your bucktail

83

down where the fish are. And there's no finer line for lake or pond fishing, where you have only minor currents to contend with and you want to sink the fly to productive depths. Then the sinker really comes into its own.

A proper leader is an invaluable part of a well-balanced outfit. It should have a heavy butt section that nearly matches the diameter of your line point, so that the energy put into the line by the forward cast carries smoothly through into the leader. The tippet should be heavy enough to turn the baitfish imitation over easily, though not heavier than is necessary. The lighter you can go on the tippet and still turn the fly over, the more success you'll have, because a light, supple tippet will insure a softer, gentle, more natural movement of the fly than a heavy tippet will allow. This will pay off in more strikes. The size of the fish you expect to hook will also have an effect on your choice of tippet size, but it's possible, and extremely enjoyable, to handle a very good fish on a very light tippet. I often fish size 10 and size 8 Thunder Creek flies on a 5X tippet. Here's where a gentle rod action helps because the rod must absorb some of the force of the strike or a fine tippet will snap. I must admit that I loose a few flies on these light tippets, but I still enjoy using them. However, most of my fishing with the smaller bucktails is done with a 4X point. As I increase the size of the fly, I also increase the strength of the tippet. As to length, I like to stay with long leaders and rarely fish a bucktail on anything shorter than nine feet, usually staying at ten feet or longer.

These remarks on tackle are, of course, mainly expressions of my own views. The selection of fishing gear is a personal thing, and what suits one fisherman may not suit another. It's like the various techniques of casting—the main idea is to get the fly to a fish in such a way as to bring on a strike, and if your casting is a bit unorthodox, don't worry about it if you catch fish and find your method easy and comfortable.

6

Fly Selection and Fishing Techniques

When it comes to selecting a Thunder Creek pattern, you will be well ahead of the game if you know, or can find out, what species of baitfish inhabit the water you are going to fish. Sometimes you won't know and won't be able to find out what forage fish are prevalent, and that's when experimentation is in order. It may still be in order even if you know what baitfish are present, for sometimes fish will be selective to one species and ignore all others. When selecting a fly at random and, when necessary, in changing flies, it pays to remember that baitfish fall into three general color categories—those with dark backs, light underparts and bright sides, those with prominent lateral stripes, and those with barred or blotchy sides. Running through an assortment of three flies with these characteristics designed into them can sometimes eliminate a lot of trials and errors and put you on the right track in a hurry.

Often the job of finding the right fly can be the most challenging aspect of the trip. One should proceed at fly selection in an orderly fashion. That's the quickest way to come up with the right answer.

The most important single consideration in fishing a Thunder Creek fly is to attempt to make the imitation act like a live fish. It has been designed to include the dominant features of a real baitfish, but the fun of bringing it to life remains for the angler. There are two basic methods of imparting action to the imitation—by using the rod tip and by stripping line. The rod tip can be used to pump the bucktail in the water and move it at varying speeds or to give it a darting action or to change its direction. The line hand can be used to strip in the line with short quick pulls that will also impart a darting motion to the fly. These two methods can be used either separately or in conjunction, but in any case it's advisable to keep the bucktail constantly working, sometimes fast, sometimes slow, but always moving and turning.

The decision of whether to fish upstream or down will be influenced somewhat by the size of the stream and the speed and depth of the current. On small, shallow streams—except in the very fastest water where line control is difficult—an upstream or quartering upstream cast is most useful. If you fish across and down in small water, the fish will constantly be spooked by your presence and by the debris that your wading kicks up. The smaller Thunder Creek flies tied on hook sizes 10 through 6 are best for the little streams because they are in line with the size of the baitfish normally found in such water. Never hesitate to try baitfish imitations in small brooks. It's a lesson I learned many years ago. I was fishing a small stream in New York State where I had always used dry flies. Nothing else seemed right for this water, and the fish usually came well to the floaters. On this outing, though, I had fished with drys most of the day without turning a fish, and in desperation I tied on a small Gray Ghost streamer. I soon discovered that there were trout in every pool and pocket and that they were hungry. One fish finally broke off the fly and it was the only one of that pattern I had, so I tied on a small Green Ghost as a second choice. I continued to catch fish though not as often as with the gray fly. Nevertheless, the lesson was well learned.

Although the upstream cast can work well on any type of water, it's much easier on medium-to-large streams to cast across or slightly upstream and allow the fly to swing down broadside to the current. Different actions can be imparted to the bucktail as you bring it back. The movement of the current can be used to advantage if you allow the fast water to catch the fly and sweep it along like an injured minnow caught up in the current. This method gives the fly plenty of action and can be deadly at times when aided by slight movements of the rod tip. If you let the current provide a good deal of the action, as suggested, you will have to mend the line periodically to keep the fly from dragging. My favorite retrieve for the across-stream cast is to work the fly with a series of rod-tip snaps upward or in a lateral direction, causing the fly to dart back toward the fisherman at a moderate speed but with a jerky motion. The rod-tip snaps should be timed so that there is a slight hesitation between each forward movement of the fly. The slack line that each snap creates is gathered in by the line hand. The hand-twist method is a good way of doing this. The line hand has to work a little faster than normal with the hand-twist retrieve, but it's not difficult to do. Try to move the fly about a foot with each rod movement. All of the action should be supplied by the rod. The line hand is used only to gather line.

It is important that you fish all the water, both fast and slow, in a systematic way, making sure that you cover all possible holding spots. Don't overlook retrieving your imitation along the edges of fast currents, sometimes bringing it back at breakneck speed. One day I watched Charlie Krom tie on a big size-2 Silver Shiner when things were particularly slow and cast it about fifty feet upstream along the edge of the current. He stripped the fly back in two-foot pulls just as fast as he could move his arm. The fly flew through the water, and it was hard to see how a fish could catch it or even intercept it. About midway through the retrieve there was a tremendous splash on the surface and Charlie was fast to a three-pound brown trout. I think he was as shocked as I was, but since then that retrieve has worked for us a good many times and is not likely to be forgotten.

Lake fishing provides a somewhat different set of challenges for the angler, but making the bucktail look alive is still the important thing to concentrate on. As lake currents are very slight, the fisherman has to supply all the action to the fly. At times he gets a little help from the wind, but more than likely the wind will be a hindrance rather than a help. I like to throw the fly out, let it sink, then retrieve it at an upward angle, trying different depths and speeds on successive casts but always making the fly act like a baitfish struggling to the surface.

Fishing a fly at depths greater than fifteen feet is difficult, even with a sinking line, and most fishing will take place much nearer the surface. It's best to fish a lake from a boat, drifting along out from the shore and casting in toward shallow water, but if that's not possible and the lake has a gentle drop off, you can wade out far enough to allow for a good backcast and can do a fairly effective job.

Fish in lakes have to move about to find their food, so a spot that's blank one minute may hold a good fish the next. However, there are always some "holding spots" in a lake. Fish tend to congregate around points of land that jut out into the water, around shoals, or where streams or springs enters the lake. The last two places are especially good after the water starts to warm up. Other good spots are along the shaded parts of the shore line where the bottom drops off sharply into several feet of water, near weed beds and large submerged logs, and among big rocks where insects and forage fish are abundant.

When a lake is turning over in the spring and fall—that is, when the layers of cold and warm water are changing positions—trout and landlocked salmon may be taken any place. At these times they are moving about at all depths in search of food. After the water stratifies (turns over), these fish seek the more comfortable thermocline (the layer of water in the 45° to 70° range) and generally cannot be taken near the surface, except sometimes during the cool of the evenings. So if you enjoy trolling with baitfish imitations, the best time to do it is while the

91

lake is turning over or soon thereafter. Warm-water species of fish can often be found near the surface all summer and can provide great fly-rod sport with the Thunder Creek series.

The usefulness of baitfish imitations in fresh water is extremely broad. You can catch almost any large fish that swims on them, except possibly some of the bottom feeders, and I'm not so sure about them. One day I took a five-pound sucker on a Marabou Shiner, and the fly was moving when he hit. I had cast upstream and was working the fly back when he inhaled it. When I set the hook he made a tremendous charge upstream and leaped gracefully out of the water. When I saw him I was sure he was the biggest brown trout in the stream, and he fought like it too. When I finally got him in, I saw that the fly was neatly hooked in his small, round mouth. The star performers on the Thunder Creek series are the trouts, landlocked salmon, and bass, but you can also have great fun catching white and yellow perch, crappies, bluegills, northern pike, and occasionally walleyes. Even the great Atlantic salmon and the musky have taken these flies. As a matter of fact, the use of baitfish imitations for Atlantic salmon is becoming more popular every year. I have seen salmon charge completely across the Cains River in New Brunswick, Canada, to grab one. Almost every place you fish, there will be some species around that are eager to take baitfish imitations.

7
Salt Water Thoughts

Salt-water fly fishing has gained an enthusiastic group of followers in recent years. It's not known exactly when fly fishing in the salt got started, and what is known about the few experiments that took place during the nineteenth century is quite vague, but it seems clear from the evidence that fresh-water fly fishing predates the salt-water variety by a good many centuries. Yet today a great number of fly fishermen took to salt-water as the last frontier where they can expect to hook big, powerful fish with any kind of regularity. What's more, salt-water flymen have proved beyond all doubt that a great variety of ocean fish will take the fly.

The waters around Florida provide many exotic species of game for the flyrodder, but some very fine fishing is also to be had all along the East and West coasts. Some of the species that have been taken successfully with the fly rod are, in no particular order, striped bass, bluefish, weakfish, mackerel, silver salmon, chinooks, bonefish, tarpon, snook, channel bass, barracuda, jacks, pompano, permit, dolphin, ladyfish, sharks, pollock, bonito, yellowtail, albacore, flounder, and for the real experts—billfish. This surely provides a wide choice, and it's not a complete list. Increasing numbers of fly fishermen who recognize the potential of salt water are willing to travel great distances to try their luck in the sea. Many anglers are even substituting trips to the sea-shore for those once-a-year or once-in-a-life-time trips that they used to take to wilderness areas. This is particularly true of those who yearn to fish Florida waters. A winter vacation in Florida can be combined with some of the greatest salt-water fly fishing and some of the most beautiful scenery to be found anywhere.

The great size and fighting ability of salt-water game fish are their principal attractions for fly fishermen. Another attraction is the fact that these fish are ravenous in their pursuit of food and feed heavily on smaller fish. Most species when on a feeding spree will hit anything that moves, especially if it looks or acts like a baitfish. Consequently, most salt-water flies are baitfish imitations, if not in actual design, at least in general action in the water. Because salt-water fish are so voracious in their feeding habits, these flies have not been refined nearly as much as their fresh-water counterparts but are rather simply and sturdily constructed. Those used along the northeastern Atlantic and the Pacific coasts tend to follow conventional fresh-water streamers and bucktails in style. The salt-water flies used in southeastern coastal waters have been given a style of their own. Generally they are made with bodies of chenille, long wings of bucktail or saddle hackle, and collars of wound hackle in a color contrasting to that of the wings. Most of these flies are brightly colored with red, yellow, white, and blue predominating. However, there have been some very successful flies designed after shrimp, eels, and other sea life. Certain of the shrimp and eel patterns look and perform like streamers and bucktails and may, at times, be mistaken for baitfish by game fish. But even taking these refinements into account, the fact remains that the possibilities of exact imitation in salt-water flies have only begun to be explored.

It was with this thought in mind that several of the fresh-water Thunder Creek patterns were first put to use in salt water. Although these patterns, the Smelt and the Silver Shiner, proved successful, it seems to me desirable that a few patterns be worked out specifically for use in the sea. Several of my friends have expermented with a striped-bass fly tied in the Thunder Creek style. It has accounted for a good number of stripers. The pattern, which has not yet been named, is as follows—hook-shank covering, silver tinsel, or even better, silver mylar tubing with the core removed; lateral stripe, bright green dyed bucktail; top of the head and back, white bucktail dyed medium blue; bottom of the head and belly, white bucktail; the eye, which is in the usual spot, is the usual yellow lacquer with black-lacquer pupil. The tying process is exactly the same as that described in Chapter 3 for fresh-water patterns, but the hook should be of a noncorroding type designed especially for salt-water use.

It appears from my observations that flies with silver hook-shank coverings, backs in various shades of blue,

95

blue-green and brown, and white underparts would come closest to successfully imitating the bright, small baitfish that abound in the ocean coastal areas. Possibly a couple of barred feathers worked into the patterns, as is done in the fresh-water Swamp Darter pattern, would give the mottled effect that's sometimes needed. It also seems desirable to coat the heads of salt-water flies with a finish more durable than lacquer. A clear epoxy glue or some other tough finish would give the flies a longer life and protect them from the teeth of salt-water game fish.

It is not my intention to go into explanations of salt-water fly fishing tackle, methods of fishing the salt, and ways of seeking out salt-water fish. There are angler-authors who have done a much better job of this than I could hope to do. But I have learned one thing, and learned it the hard way—a short wire leader is a very desirable item. Salt-water game fish have sharp teeth and powerful jaws. Otherwise, the chances are good that if you are not already a salt-water fly fisherman, your heaviest fresh-water equipment will be adequate to do the job in the salt. Give it a try. You won't be sorry.

8

Assuring the Future of Your Sport

s far as the fly fisherman is concerned, good water management is a matter of self-preservation. Our sport cannot continue unless sportsmen themselves show genuine concern and take an aggressive part in the conservation and improvement of water resources. Most of us are aware of the problems we face in order to assure the future of fly fishing, but we often have a tendency to leave them for the other guy to take care of. There are far too few fisherman who are willing to participate on an active basis in the efforts necessary to save, and perhaps even to improve, our sport-fishing resources. Too many of us fail to consider water management in its broader senses but think of it solely in terms of stream-improvement—the physical work of jockeying rocks, logs, and the like to improve water movement. Certainly this type of work enters into the picture, and it must be done, but it is neither the most important part of the problem nor the most difficult to accomplish.

Water quality must come first; there can be no game fish without it. And without public access to first-quality water, there will still be no fishing for the average angler. To guarantee these essentials the fisherman must keep a constant vigil. This is not as burdensome a responsibility as it may sound, for there are many little things of great importance that any angler can accomplish on his own, without fanfare and even without belonging to any kind of a conservation club. Even so, membership in a soundly organized and well-run club that has been established to look after the interests of the angler is an excellent way to help guarantee your future as a fly fisherman. Such clubs are especially effective in dealing with the political aspects of conservation problems.

The political aspects of conservation efforts are the most difficult to deal with and most of the problems in the conservation field are affected by political considerations. The only effective way of dealing with such situations is by presenting a united front, and this is best done by joining a strongly motivated club—one that isn't afraid to affiliate with similar clubs—and then taking an active part. But consider also a few of the things you can do by yourself. For example, when you see something happening at a favorite fishing spot that is causing or will cause deterioration of the water, report the situation to the proper authorities. State Conservation authorities, water-shed authorities, and private-ownership interests are always anxious to hear of abuses that take place in their areas of interest. These people cannot be everywhere and are happy to have your assistance. In the case of public ownership, the officials can then carry out their responsibilities to the public; in the case of private ownership, the owners are usually very eager to protect their investments, and such aid to private owners will also help solve the access problem. In any event, you are protecting the future of your sport. It's a good idea, too, once a report has been made, to follow up the consequences and make certain that your effort caused some action. If nothing was done after your first report, make a second inquiry. Repeated inquiries will probably bring action. Don't become discouraged. Your future sport is at stake.

Here's an incident that happened recently in New York state. A contractor was putting up a few homes adjacent to a fine little public trout stream. After the construction site had been cleared, the surface water from the construction area and the road beds found its way into the stream, dragging with it a great amount of sand and silt. The trout began disappearing fast, fishing fell off sharply, and the stream was left in an unsightly mess. The fishermen that frequented the stream did nothing but complain—all but one, that is. This one responsible angler initiated the action with the proper authorities, and several members of the Theodore Gordon Flyfishers provided the follow through. A satisfactory solution to the problem was reached in very short order. The contractor installed an adequate silting basin, which allowed the solid material in the run-off water to filter out before the water was discharged into the stream. The stream, which has since been flushed out several times by high water, has now nearly returned to its former self, and fishing is as good as ever. No great

99

effort was required here by the fisherman, just genuine concern over the future of one of his favorite streams. The important thing to note is that one fisherman saw an abuse and made an effort to correct it. Think what could be accomplished nationwide if we all donated a few minutes to report destructive situations on our lakes, streams, and seashores and to let the officials know we are concerned.

There are even simpler things we can do to help our cause. We have all gone fishing and run across bits of trash and debris in the water, along the shores, or scattered along woodland trails. Why not pick up a tin can or a piece of paper on the way home and drop it in the car trunk to be properly disposed of later? We will always have those among us who are careless or who couldn't care less about discarding lunch wrappers, cans and, yes, even sometimes the week's garbage or an old sofa. And even the most dedicated fly fishermen sometimes forget to pick up after themselves. Let's face the facts. We don't want to turn ourselves into refuse collectors when we would rather be fishing, but we should take time to report to law-enforcement agencies such large abuses as willful trash dumping in stream areas. Fishermen usually get blamed for these situations, but I know of several cases in which sifting of trash turned up the names of local residents and as a result fines were imposed on the dumpers under statutes covering health standards. Some of the little problems, though, can be handled very quietly if enough fishermen help. You'll be surprised at the feeling of satisfaction you get by setting a good example, and it's a habit that can catch on with other fishermen.

There are many things you can do to help the cause. And to repeat, it doesn't take a great deal of effort or time; it just requires an awareness of the problem and a willingness to spend a few minutes helping to correct the situation. When you do your part, you are helping to assure your future as a fly fisherman.

DRESSINGS FOR THE THUNDER CREEK SERIES

NAME	HOOK SHANK COVERING	LATERAL STRIPE	TOP OF HEAD AND BACK	BOTTOM OF HEAD AND BELLY	EYE
Primary Patterns					
Blacknose Dace*	silver tinsel	black bucktail	brown bucktail	white bucktail	yellow lacquer with black dot
Emerald Shiner	fluorescent green floss with silver tinsel rib or green tinsel	none	"	"	"
Golden Shiner	yellow tinsel	yellow bucktail	brown bucktail or brown part of a green or blue bucktail	"	"
Marabou Shiner	silver tinsel	none	silver-pheasant crest feather	white marabou	"
Rainbow Trout	"	pink bucktail	brown part of bucktail dyed green	white bucktail	"
Redfin Shiner	pink or red fluorescent floss, silver tinsel rib	none	brown bucktail	"	"

Species				
Silver Shiner	silver tinsel	none	"	"
Smelt	silver tinsel	orchid bucktail	"	"
Spottail Shiner	black floss caudal spot, gold tinsel	none	brown part of bucktail dyed green	"
Strawcolor Shiner	silver tinsel	blue bucktail	brown part of bucktail dyed pink	"
Secondary Patterns				
Redlip Shiner	black floss tail, black floss with gold tinsel rib, orange-floss fins	pale-yellow bucktail	black bucktail	pale-yellow bucktail
Steelcolor Shiner	blue fluorescent floss, silver tinsel rib	none	brown part of bucktail dyed blue	pale-yellow bucktail
Striped Jumprock	gold tinsel	pale-orange bucktail	dark brown to black bucktail	pale-orange bucktail
Swamp Darter	silver tinsel	two grizzly saddle hackles	brown bucktail	white bucktail
Wedgespot Shiner	black floss caudal spot, black floss, silver tinsel rib	two strands of brown floss	light-brown bucktail	white bucktail

*See special details in text for head markings.